Devotions
for a
New Mother

BETHANY HOUSE BOOKS
by Mildred Tengbom

Devotions for a New Mother
Grief for a Season

Mildred Tengbom

Devotions
for a
New Mother

BETHANY HOUSE
Minneapolis, Minnesota

Library of Congress Cataloging-in-Publication Data

Tengbom, Mildred.
  [Life to cherish]
  Devotions for a new mother : insights, meditations, and prayers from a mother's heart / by Mildred Tengbom.— Rev. ed.
      p. cm.
    ISBN 0-7642-2598-7 (alk. paper)
1. Mothers—Prayer-books and devotions—English. I. Title.
    BV283.M7 T46 2002
    242'.6431—dc21   2001005707

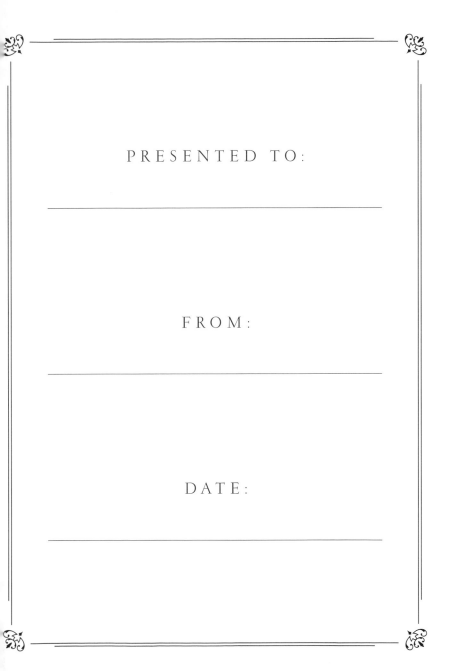

PRESENTED TO:

FROM:

DATE:

Mildred Tengbom is mother to two sons and two daughters. During her adventurous life she has lived in the Himalayas on the eastern border of Nepal, on the lower slopes of Mt. Kilimanjaro in Tanzania, on the island state of Singapore, and in the United States. She has written twenty books and continues to write and teach writing. She and her husband reside in Claremont, California.

A Word From
the Author

Environment does make a difference. The atmosphere we as parents provide can do much toward making our children become the kind of persons they will be. We hold awesome power in our hands. We actually can do much to shape our children.

All of us want socially well-adjusted, happy children, who can find their niche in life and make their own unique contributions. What then can we do specifically toward accomplishing these goals?

First, we can cultivate a strong relationship of love and trust between our children and us. This is important if our children are going to experience full social growth. Our children must know we love them. They also need to learn to respond to our love. If children do not experience love and learn to respond to it, later in life they will tend to use people to their advantage.

A solid relationship of love and trust is necessary for intellectual learning as well. Happy children learn easily. Unhappy children are usually full of fears and anxieties, self-doubt and low self-esteem; all of these thwart and hinder intellectual growth and stifle curiosity and creativity.

Second, we can provide a stable home atmosphere where love unites everyone. This does not mean that there will never be struggles or tension or disagreements. But it means that children will see how differences are reconciled and peace is maintained or restored. The home can be the school where children learn the art of getting along with others.

But children also need the security of a stable home and freedom from anxiety that their parents will separate and one of them will abandon them.

Third, we can encourage our children to learn. Children will learn only if adults will grant them the freedom to satisfy their natural curiosity. Let us stimulate their quest. Encourage it. Join them in their explorations and discoveries through mobiles, pictures, books, music, rich language, questions, observations, and interaction with other people.

Devotions for a New Mother was written to reflect the kind of atmosphere in which children can flourish and grow into happy, well-adjusted, caring, and productive persons. We hope it also reflects the joy of parenthood. That joy has been ours. We wish it for you too.

Contents

Behold, children are a gift of the Lord;
The fruit of the womb is a reward.

Psalm 127:3 NASB

1

I Walk the Beach at Twilight

Here on the beach it's quiet and refreshing and I can think. The breakers washing in, the sea gulls dipping and flying overhead, the dark gray clouds, heavy with rain, moving up from the horizon, the wind whipping my hair, the salty mist stinging my face—all help to clear my mind.

Sometimes, Father, I feel overwhelmed. Life has become so complex. Demand after demand pushes its way into my life. I have become so many people, owing allegiance and loyalty and love to so many others that momentarily I become confused and need to turn to you for a sure word of direction again.

I am a wife, the chosen helpmeet of a wonderful man. And I am in the process of becoming a mother, a co-creator with God and my husband of an individual whose life I must mold, not only for this life but also for eternity. The awe and wonder of it fill my soul.

I also realize that as a citizen of this vast, beautiful, and rich country in which I live, I have certain responsibilities that go along with the privilege.

Absorbed as I am in the lives of others, something deep within never lets me forget that I am a unique individual, endowed by you with certain distinctive gifts and abilities given to me that I might contribute to the happiness and welfare of those around me.

Most important of all—and I never cease to wonder at it—I am your child, Father. I thank you for the sacrifice of your Son that made this relationship possible. Fellowship with you brings life into focus, keeps me from despair, puts courage in my heart, and gives me the faith to trust you for the best outcome in all of life.

Here on the beach, when I lift my eyes toward the vast heavens above me and consider interstellar space, I want to kneel and worship you. When the frothy waves wash over my bare feet, pushing the sand between my toes, reminding me that their boundaries have been set, I want to fling out my arms in joy that you, God, are in control. And when I turn my back to the sea and face the city, where the evening lights are beginning to twinkle, though my heart weeps with yours that so many thousands are estranged from you, I thank you that you are their Savior, and that you love them and you care.

I want to understand what is important to my husband and to help him realize his goals.

I want to be able to listen to our children, to understand them and to love them. Not in a selfish, grasping way, but in a way that will help them to be all you want them to be.

I care about those in the city too: the smug, self-satisfied ones who don't think they need you; the frustrated, angry ones; the lonely and the homeless; the children of divorced homes; the students in the colleges and universities; the homesick students from overseas; the forgotten older people; and all those who have left their homelands for whatever reason to join us here.

But caring is not enough. Even as John and I prepare to welcome a little one into our home, show us also how we can reach out to others. We need to hear your voice so we can understand what you want us, as individuals, to do.

That's why I'm walking the beach tonight, Father.

In this busy world of ours, help me to be wise. I hold in my hands your Word. Help me to keep it in my heart. Instruct me through it.

In the quietness of this twilight hour, speak to me.

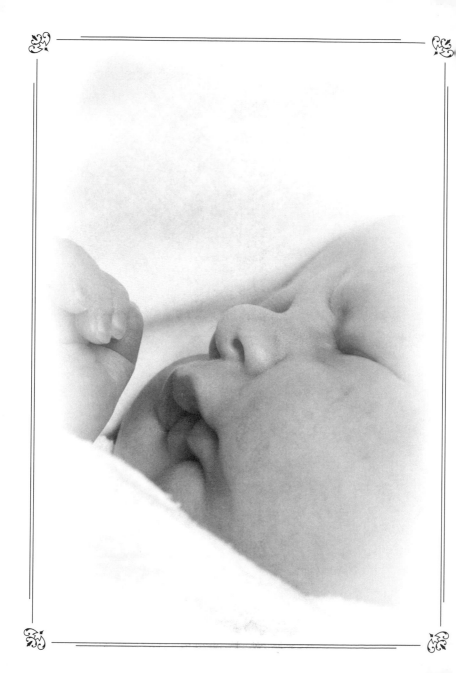

2

The First Stirrings of My Baby Within Me

I woke up last night. Something was different.

I lay motionless, wondering.

Then a gentle wave rippled across my belly.

I pressed my fingers against it and felt the flesh move again like a quiet, full swell on a summer lake. The kind that gently rocks an anchored boat.

Somehow in that moment my baby became real to me.

With my other hand I reached over to run my fingers through my husband's hair.

"Hmmm?"

"Guess what?" I guided his hand to the top of mine. We lay in the dark, quiet, waiting. After what seemed like a very long time there was another faint ripple and then a sudden movement that startled my husband.

He chuckled. "He'll make a good football player," he said contentedly and rolled over to sleep.

I was too excited to sleep. The awe of bringing another human being into the world captivated me.

To create is a basic human need.

We busy ourselves with arts and crafts and other skills.

We build houses, churches, bridges, and freeways.

We cook, bake, and decorate our homes.

We design and sew, knit and crochet.

We paint and sculpt.

We compose music.

But to be a co-creator with God of a human being who will breathe and move, walk and talk, express emotions—and know God! What could compare with that?

I think about what our child will be like. He or she will be part me, part my husband, part of many who have gone before us, and yet a unique person.

God, thank you for allowing us to share with you the joy and wonder of a new life.

As our child grows, help us to remember this little one is not only ours but yours.

Enable us to give our child the freedom to become the distinct person you desire him or her to be. We have dreams for our child, but if our child does not share our dreams, help us to let him go.

At the same time, dear God, watch over our dear one. Don't let our child miss the best you have for him—or is it "her"?

Perfect your work in our child. You are the trustworthy, all-wise God.

3

Does My Husband Know How Much I Need Him?

Having a baby is a new experience for me.

What will it be like?

Sometimes, especially at night, I am afraid.

I wish I could reach over and awaken my husband and ask him to put his arms around me. I know I'd feel better. I wonder if he knows how much I need him.

Last night I awakened afraid again and wondered about whether having a baby would hurt much. Will I be able to bear the pain? What if our baby is born blind? Or deaf? What if she has some incurable disease? What if—

I moved closer to John for comfort. He woke up and took me into his strong arms.

I cried a little and told him about all my fears.

He smoothed my hair back and kissed away my tears—and fears.

"I needed you, John," I said. "I'm so glad you're here for me."

"I'm glad too," he said, kissing me again. "Sometimes I've felt so useless. You seem to be going through this alone, and I want to know how I can help. Thanks for sharing your fears with me."

I felt so warm and peaceful and cared for. I knew everything was going to be all right. Soon we were both asleep.

4

What Will Our Baby Be Like?

My baby becomes more and more real to me each day. After my husband is off to work, I feel like my baby is my only companion. But that's okay. I'm beginning to enjoy the company.

I think so much about what he or she will be like! It won't be long before I'll know if he is a redhead, a blond, or dark-haired. Or if she has freckles. (Do babies *have* freckles?)

I know his eyes will probably start out blue and change, if they are going to, between three and six months. If it's a girl, will she have a pixie nose and a dimpled chin? If it's a boy, will he look like his daddy and be a wonderful older brother someday?

It'll take longer to discover what my baby's personality is like. Extroverted? Sanguine? Or quiet, pensive, reflective. Maybe even shy and indecisive.

When my husband felt the baby move again last night, he repeated his prediction, "He's going to be a great football player."

"What makes you so sure?" I asked. "She could be a school-teacher or a librarian."

"A...what?" he gasped, leaning forward in his chair.

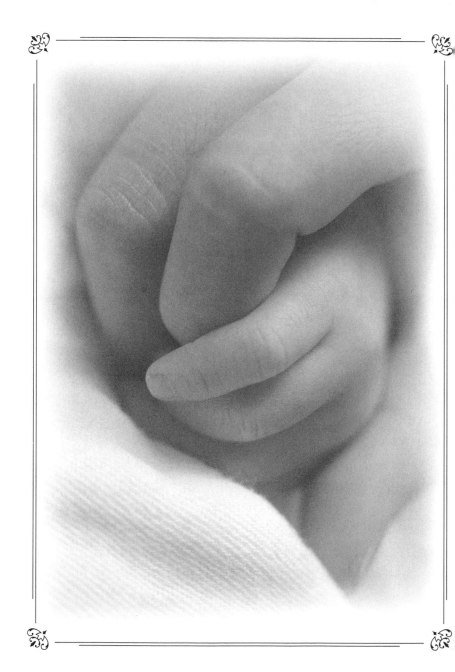

"A schoolteacher or a librarian," I repeated calmly. "My father loves books, you remember."

John snorted. "What does that have to do with anything?"

I'm afraid we could have a little problem, Lord. What if we have a son and he doesn't want to be a football player? We may have to sit down and talk this over. But maybe I'm getting ahead of myself. A career for our baby, or even what sport he or she plays is quite a ways off. But it is a little frightening to think about guiding a child and helping him or her make wise decisions. I feel so inadequate. We'll need your wisdom, Lord. Meet our needs so we will be able to meet our baby's needs.

5

If Two Are Not Enough, There Are Three

My friend Cheryl has lost her baby.
I can hardly believe it.
We talked of how much fun we'd have with babies
    only months apart.
We never considered the possibility of losing
    one of them.
It happens more often than we think.
I feel cold and clammy,
    like I did when as a child
    in the winter
    I used to stay out and play too long
    in the snow after
    the sun had diminished, and the fierce cold
    penetrated my bones.
I feel numb,
    like all my limbs have gone to sleep and refuse
    to function.
I'm afraid too.

What if it happens to us?
I voiced my fears to my husband.
He held me close and for a long time said nothing.
When he spoke, he said,
"Before we married we agreed
that even if we were not blessed with children,
we still wanted to be together,
and that alone would be enough."
But my love for this unborn child has grown so much
these past months.
I couldn't imagine losing this baby.
I wound my arms around my husband's neck,
and buried my face in his shoulder
    and sobbed.
"Hold me tight, my love,
    and reassure me,
so I'll know again
that just being together,
the two of us sharing our lives,
could be enough."
He whispered tenderly into my hair,
"Maybe just the two of us *isn't* enough.
But we have God."
And my nervous fears were quieted.

6

How Was It for Mary?

Last night sudden pains awoke me.
"False labor," the doctor called it, when they
    didn't persist.
Mixed feelings chased up and down the corridors of
    my heart
    when those pains began.
Excitement—like when it was my turn to step onstage
    for the school play.
Joy—like having Christmas finally come.
Anticipation and curiosity—like when I was about to open
    the big mysterious package from Aunt Jane.
And a little apprehension and fear—like when we hear the
    tornado warning sirens.
Is it normal to feel a little afraid?
I wonder if Jesus' mother, Mary, was afraid too.
In fact, I've often wondered how it was for Mary.
Especially that last day of the long journey to Bethlehem.
Our Lord was her first child.
She most likely had a long labor.
The day he was born, she and Joseph probably went

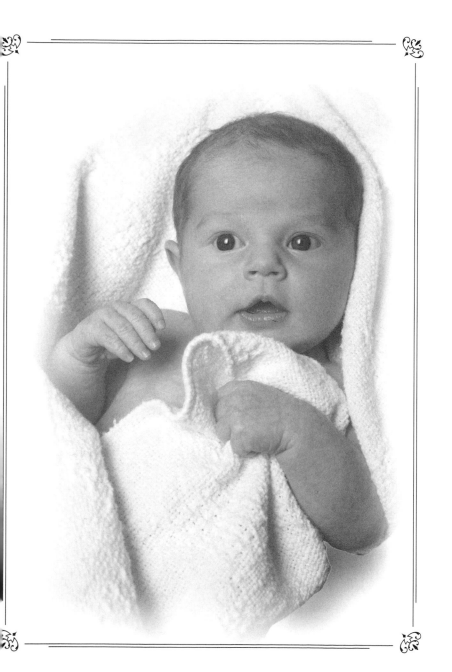

from Jericho
up to Jerusalem
and then across to Bethlehem.
It's seven to ten miles from Jerusalem to Bethlehem,
    depending on the route.
That means the pains very likely had begun
    while Mary was in Jerusalem,
    if not before.
Her older cousin, Elizabeth, lived in the suburbs.
Elizabeth knew Mary's secret,
    and had just given birth to a child.
Strange that Mary didn't stop at Elizabeth's.
Did she know the Scripture that said the Messiah was
    to be born in David's city?
Was she beginning to understand?
Or was she still wondering and pondering?
What made her continue the journey when the pains
    became intense?
How was it for her on the way?
Did she cringe when the pains came in earnest?
Did she double up on the donkey's back,
    gripping the mane
    in sheer panic?
Those giant rolling hills.
The winding, stony path.
And then it was getting dark.
Did her anxiety grow with the darkening sky?

So far from home!
So far from her mother!
Joseph plodded on, leading the donkey;
unaware of her pain but nervous, nonetheless.
Where and when would this child be born?
And what did Joseph know about delivering babies?
Out of the darkness a shadow loomed.
It was a stone monument.
"Rachel's tomb," Joseph said almost reverently.
And Mary remembered.
Rachel had been on safari too when her pains began.
Her baby lived.
But Rachel died.
"Please, Joseph, let's keep going!"

It's normal to be a little fearful, isn't it? I keep remembering the words of the angels, "Don't be afraid!" And I know you told your disciples many times not to be afraid. But sometimes I am. Help me to trust you more.

7

Learning to Relax

Tension.

I never realized before how tense I was until I began these
exercises to help me relax.

I want to be able to give birth more easily.

"Tense your finger, now consciously relax it," the
instructions read. "Let it go limp. Drop it.
Feel your arched back relax and sink into the pad
under it. Let your hunched-up shoulders drop and
rest them completely on the pad. Full force."

As I go through the exercises, I'm even learning to drop off
to sleep for a few minutes.

But it's not just a matter of learning how to relax muscles.

It helps to understand what makes them tighten in the first
place.

Fear and worry string me taut.

My doctor is helping.

He has given me books that explain clearly what
will be happening in my body.

At every appointment he allows time for me to ask
questions.

He has assured me I can take something if the pain
becomes more than I can bear.
I think I have a good doctor.
My mother has been helpful too.
She's so realistic.
She doesn't deny the pain,
but assures me that
women are built to bear pain.
In fact, she goes beyond that.
She says a certain fierce exultation and triumph
can come from pain
when you know it's productive.
So my doctor's explanations of what will happen
physically,
and my mother's reassurance that I will find emotional
and spiritual strength,
have been putting my fears to rest.
My husband will be with me too,
and there's nothing that comforts me more than having
him with me.
Yet even with all this help,
I still have fleeting moments of fear.
At those times I turn to God's Word:

"My grace is sufficient for you" (2 Corinthians 12:9).

"Never will I leave you; never will I forsake you"
(Hebrews 13:5).

"Cast all your anxiety on him because he cares for you"
(1 Peter 5:7).

*"I am leaving you with a gift—peace of mind and heart!
And the peace I give isn't fragile like the peace the world
gives. So don't be troubled or afraid"* (John 14:27 TLB).

*"You will keep in perfect peace him whose mind is steadfast,
because he trusts in you. Trust in the Lord forever, for the Lord, the
Lord, is the Rock eternal"* (Isaiah 26:3–4).

*"Do not worry about anything, but pray and ask God for
everything you need, always giving thanks. And God's peace, which
is so great we cannot understand it, will keep your hearts and
minds in Christ Jesus"* (Philippians 4:6–7 NCV).

*"I am the Lord your God, who holds your right hand, and I
tell you, 'Don't be afraid. I will help you' "* (Isaiah 41:13 NCV).

*"Don't be afraid, because I have saved you. I have called you by
name, and you are mine. When you pass through the waters, I will
be with you. When you cross rivers, you will not drown. When you*

walk through fire, you will not be burned, nor will the flames hurt you" (Isaiah 43:1–2 NCV).

"He takes care of his people like a shepherd. He gathers them like lambs in his arms and carries them close to him. He gently leads the mothers of the lambs" (Isaiah 40:11 NCV).

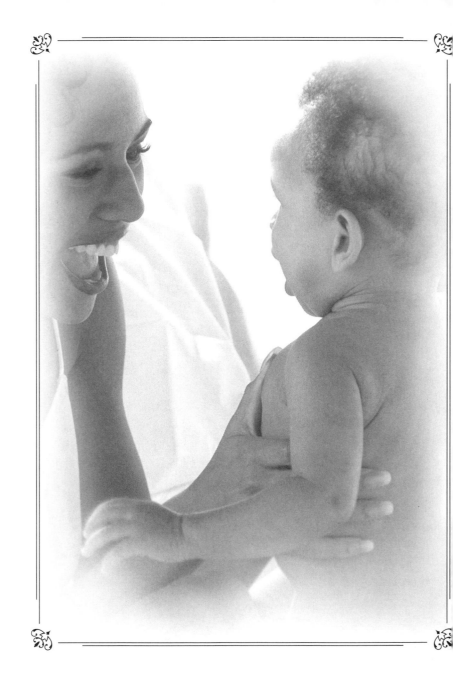

8

God, My Deliverer

These days when I feel my belly swell and move with life,
    and my little one within kicks with reckless abandon,
I feel so close to you, God.
How often in the Bible you identify with mothers and
    describe your own loving care and concern in mothers'
    language.
You are the One who gently leads the toddler, coaxing the
    hesitant, fearful one to walk.
You are the One who covers the wounds and kisses the
    hurts away.
You are the One who gives the hungry, squalling infant
    nourishment, soothing and comforting the restless
    (see Hosea 11:1–11; Isaiah 66:13).
You describe your own birth pangs (see Isaiah 42:14)
    and your faithfulness to not forget your child (see
    Isaiah 49:15).
    Sometimes you refer to yourself as the One who
    assists in the birth, bringing forth the child
    (see Psalm 22:9-10; Psalm 71:6).
This role means everything to me now.

Oh, God! Be my tender, understanding, skillful Assistant
    when my hour comes!

Sit by my bed.

Hold my hand.

Speak reassuringly to me as only you can.

You know my frame; you know what I can bear.

Give me courage.

Calm my anxious fears.

Refresh me with a cool cloth on my forehead and ice
    on my parched lips.

Hold me tightly if I tremble with uncertainty.

Stand beside me that I may draw strength from you to
    deliver this child safely.

Stay by my side; don't leave me alone.

Coach me in my breathing,
    encourage me to relax
    and to rest between contractions.

Oh, God, you are a compassionate God,
    who describes yourself as the one who brings the child
    forth from the womb.

How glad I am that you will be with me.

9

I Was Called to Sing

I found a poem this morning, my little unborn one, which expresses how I feel as I carry you within me and know you are growing and developing every day:

> I was called to dance,
> I was called to sing.
> Here I start to sway,
> here I start to swing
> to heavenly, heavenly music.
>
> As the mountains leap
> and the trees applaud,
> I will run and laugh,
> I will shout and laud
> my heavenly, heavenly Maker.
>
> I can see His step,
> I can hear His voice.
> Earth proclaims His praise.
> Cloud and clod rejoice
> on this heavenly, heavenly morning.

Nothing can alarm,
        Nothing can destroy,
as I enter in
        amidst His kingdom's joy
        in one heavenly, heavenly moment.

—Kerstin Holmlund

The greatest wonder of all came when I discovered that the poet, because of the crippling of rheumatoid arthritis, has not been able to stand for eight years!

Oh, my precious unborn child! I cherish for your father, for you, and for me, that courageous dancing spirit that sings its way through life, in joy, in sorrow, in health, in disabling illness, in success, or in disappointment.

10

The Comparison Game

I shouldn't have been upset, but I must admit I was.

My doctor released me from the hospital only two days after my baby was born because my mother would be here to help me. I had been home only about an hour when the doorbell rang.

Our neighbor's thirteen-year-old son was standing outside. "Can I see your baby?"

What could I say? "Sure, come in."

As he peered into the crib he sucked in his breath through his teeth. "Wow! Sure looks funny, doesn't he? All red and wrinkly like an old man. Hey, you!" he said, thrusting a grubby finger into the tiny fist of my brand-new baby. "He sure isn't very good-looking, is he," he said cheerfully, blowing a big bubble with the gum he chewed noisily.

I choked back the words I wanted to say, and instead said, "Give him time."

After a few awkward moments, the boy left, and as I closed the door behind him, I turned to see my mother looking at me with an amused expression.

"It's not easy to take, is it," she said. "But I'm afraid it's only the beginning."

"The beginning of what?"

"Of your baby being evaluated by others. People more often than not say what they think. He'll always be compared to someone else. That's life in a competitive world."

"What do you mean, Mother?" I didn't like what I was hearing.

"Well, people observe how you do things, how you care for your baby. They will ask if he sleeps through the night, if he's getting enough to eat, if you don't think he needs a supplemental bottle, if the doctor thinks he's gaining enough weight. It goes on and on. You just have to take it in stride. Sometimes people have good advice, and sometimes they just like to talk." Mother sighed. "Of course, this is mild compared to when he starts school—"

Mother scooped the new little clothes out of the washer and tossed them into the dryer.

"It's hard to know how much to expect of each child," she sighed. "And it's hard for parents not to compare even their own children, one with another."

The enormity of the task ahead of me, of bringing up my child unscarred through all this, frightened me.

"You compared me too, Mom, with Julie!" (Somehow my older sister was endowed with all the gifts: pretty face, intellect, charm, clear skin, lovely hair—at least that's the way I've always felt.)

My remark sent a pained look across my mother's face. I wished I hadn't said anything.

"I'm sorry," she said, brushing back a stray wisp of hair. "It was wrong of me to do that. Did I really make comparisons?" She shook her head. "I do appreciate you so much! Your thoughtfulness, your concern for others, your easygoing nature. I don't know why it takes us so long to learn how to accept our children as they are and appreciate their good points. Maybe it's because we're so slow to accept and like ourselves."

"I was skinny and bony," she remembered. "Flat-footed, they called me at school. Your Aunt Theresa was always telling me how dumb I was. I began to believe it." She checked the new little clothes in the dryer. "It was your father who helped me begin to believe in myself. He has been wonderful!" A smile creased her mouth, and her blue eyes were shining.

"Attitudes have a way of being passed on from family to family and from generation to generation," she continued. "It can be both fortunate and unfortunate—depending." She folded my baby's soft new things and carried them into the nursery. When she came back she put her arms around me. I found myself relaxing and laid my head on her shoulder.

"I love you, hon," she said simply. "And I do wish I'd begun to enjoy you much sooner, when you were very young." She stroked my hair. "Maybe you can learn from my mistakes. Accept your little one as he is and love him unconditionally. Take what others say about him with a grain of salt, and turn up your nose at judgmental remarks about your care for him. I know you will do your very best."

The advice about turning up my nose was so unexpected coming from my mother that I laughed out loud.

She released her gentle hold on me. "You rest now, while I straighten up the house. We want everything to be pleasant and in order when John comes home to his wife and new baby son."

11

Don't Eat Me Up!

My but you've been hungry today, my little one.

You just grabbed at me when I cuddled you close. And it hurt!

A mother's breasts are sensitive, don't you know?

You don't need to tug so hard, as if you would eat me up!

But I'm glad you're hungry. I love your hearty cry.

It tells me you're fully alive. Wondrously alive! Strong! Determined! Ready to take on the world!

How grateful I am for this.

I remember a friend whose baby came two months early. He weighed only four pounds. He was small enough to be cradled in his daddy's strong hand.

And how sleepy he was—as though he resented being brought into this cold, cruel world so soon. He wanted to just curl up and sleep cozily and tightly wrapped as though still in the safe, warm protection of his mother's womb.

"Feed him every two hours," the doctor ordered my friend.

What a job it was for her. She had to snap the bottoms of his feet to keep him awake. His little head would droop to the

side, and he would be asleep after a few seconds of nursing.

She tapped his cheek and tugged on his little chin to get him to continue sucking.

Sometimes it took forty-five minutes to get him to nurse twenty minutes.

And then two hours later she had to start all over again. How wonderful it was after two months to have him wake up on his own and cry for his food.

He had suddenly come alive!

So I guess it's okay to tug on me, to "eat me up." I'm so glad you're strong and well and hungry!

I hope you'll have the same eager, insatiable thirst for God someday.

Nothing will please your dad and me more.

"Zeal for your house consumes me" (Psalm 69:9). The disciples recalled those prophetic words about Jesus as they watched Him at work, doing what He believed His Father wanted Him to do.

How wonderful if you exhibit the same zeal, my little one, being taken up with God and His work and His people—full of vision, loving God so passionately that no sacrifice will be too great. I desire this for you.

I know that the one who gives himself completely and wholeheartedly to God and to His work in the world will be greatly rewarded.

Our needy world needs men and women who have an insatiable thirst for God. I pray that you will be one of these, my child. God will rejoice in your zest for life even as I do now.

12

Diapering

If I had had younger brothers or sisters to help care for when I was young, wouldn't I have been better equipped for changing diapers and bathing a baby now?

The first time I was totally unprepared; I really thought I wouldn't make it! But my mother assured me I would get used to it.

Oddly enough, now I feel that changing my baby's diapers is the most meaningful way I can show my love for him. He is totally dependent on me. The care I give brings comfort to him. If I neglected him, he would be very uncomfortable and even develop a rash or painful sores. And the very fact that the task is sometimes unpleasant contributes to its being a ministry of love. It's my way of telling my child I love him no matter what.

This is the way God loves me—*completely*—no strings attached. How offensive I must be to Him in my selfishness, pride, and stubbornness. Unlovely. Unattractive. Even repulsive. But He loves me and accepts me as I am—in my weakness, my failings, and my utter dependence.

So as I lovingly bathe you, change you, clothe you, I feel that

I am showing my deep love for you, just as God has shown His deep love for me—anytime and all the time.

Lord Jesus, thank you for loving me completely—just as I am.

13

Hang in There, Baby

Sometimes I feel like a scrawny shrub tenaciously clinging to the side of a cliff, sending my roots down deep to draw nourishment from the soil and hanging on lest I be plunged into the river below.

The first few days after you were born, I felt so bubbly and enthusiastic about being a mom. My heart sang praises all day long. But now, suddenly, I've felt so…deflated. Let down. In fact, I am feeling discouraged and even depressed.

There doesn't seem to be an obvious reason.

"Don't worry," Mother said last night when I talked to her. "It often happens to young mothers. It doesn't have anything to do with your love for your husband or your baby. It's a hormone imbalance, a chemical upset in your body. If it persists, see your doctor. But it might just pass quickly."

Days like this will come for you too, my little one.

"Man is born to trouble as surely as sparks fly upward" (Job 5:7), a wise old man declared centuries ago.

And he was right. We all need to recognize that a measure of trouble is the lot of every man, woman, and child.

I hope I can bring you up so that you are prepared for trouble and learn to embrace it. The people of our culture avoid pain and discomfort whenever possible. We protect and shield and complain about even small inconveniences.

Our frustration level is low.

And then when we don't practice in life's little surprise quizzes, we fail in the big exam.

Human emotions are so fickle. They ebb and flow. Soar and descend. Sing and sigh.

How good to know we need not be dependent on how we feel.

The important thing is that I am connected securely to someone I can trust. My roots have gone into the Rock, Christ Jesus. From Him I draw daily, hourly, sustenance for every need, no matter how discouraged I might feel or how inadequate to care for my baby.

Jesus loves me. He cares for me, for us. He sustains me. He forgives, strengthens, enables, and supports me—and you. All our needs are met in Him.

So blow, winds! Descend, dark clouds of depression. You may smother happiness for a while, but you are not the victor.

Down times are part of life—to be embraced, to learn from.

How else will I grow strong?

How else will I be able to teach you, my child?

For precepts will be only hollow echoes if you do not see me tenaciously clinging to the Rock.

14

Easing Into
Responsibility

My mother went home today.

"Stay a few days longer," I pleaded.

"No, I think you will be fine," she assured me. "You're feeling good. Your baby is healthy. John is with you in the evenings and on the weekends. You don't need me anymore right now."

"You don't think so?"

"No; I think it's time you stretch yourself and see what you can do on your own with your new little family."

I walked with her to the car. As she was leaving, she rolled down the window and said, "If you *really* need me, just call. I'm only an hour away."

She was right to leave when she did.

Bringing up this baby is our responsibility—John's and mine, not hers. And we'll manage somehow.

I'm glad that over the years Mom has eased me into accepting responsibility. I don't think it came easily for her; she's such a leader, an organizer, and so efficient.

But when I was seventeen and through with high school, she let me go. The first couple of years I followed the usual path of conformity, combining college and work. But then the wanderlust bit me, and for the next two years I traversed the country: Seattle, San Francisco, Los Angeles, Detroit, New York, Philadelphia, and Toronto. I joined a Christian commune. I wonder what she thought all those years. But she never said a word about my choices, only welcomed me home whenever I returned.

I grew a lot during those years. I looked for bargains whenever I shopped, and I learned to do without.

I was surrounded by friends who accepted me as I was and loved me; I began to like myself and to develop self-confidence.

The values I adopted then have followed me ever since, and I still feel good about them.

I learned to get along with other people—perhaps one of life's most difficult lessons.

And I learned to turn myself over to God and to trust Him to lead and direct me. I wonder if this ever would have happened if my mother hadn't released me.

Then John and I got married. We've made it through our first years, and we'll make it okay with our first baby.

Lord, it was great having Mother here for a few days when I really needed her. Thank you for her. Thank you for her assurance that she is always on call when I need her. Help me to be a good mother, so Mom will be able to see in me her reward for all she has taught me.

15

Contentment at the Close of the Day

We sit together at the close of the day,
together in our family room,
the three of us together, yet apart.
The fire crackles in the fireplace,
    the hungry flames curling around the logs,
    little puffs of smoke spiraling upward.
We are cozy and content.
We are a family.
We are complete.
No one has to speak; we are together.
Our new baby is asleep in the basket.
Occasionally I hear little grunts and mutterings,
    snorts and stirrings.
It's a contented sound.
What do babies dream of?
I sit curled up in the big chair, writing notes.
My husband is hunched over his desk scratching comments
    on the term papers he's evaluating.

We are together, a family.
We sit together, yet apart.
I like this feeling of togetherness.
We are content and warm and happy.
Thank you, Lord.

16

I Need a Break!

I can hardly wait for my husband to come home.
I've just about had it.
If I can't hand this baby over to someone and get away
from the crying for a little while, *I'll* cry—or scream.

On days like this I need special help from you, God.
I need to be sensitive to my husband's needs too.
Sometimes his day's been really tough,
and when he comes home
he only wants
    a welcome kiss,
    a cup of hot coffee,
    (something home-baked would be nice),
    and solitude
for half an hour,
to help him unwind,
    let go of his frustrations,
    and settle down.
I've learned if I rush in on those days

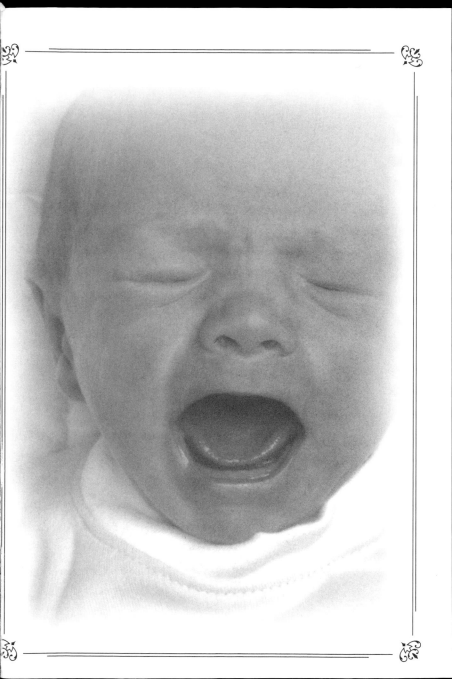

and unload my troubles

or just chatter about my day,

we're both soon upset,

or pacing out our words in even, low-pitched tones:

"Can't you let me be alone for a while?" he asks

(he who married me so we could be together).

"You don't understand me!" I challenge

(I who thought her husband would always understand).

False expectations both!

So today give me extra understanding and patience, Lord.

If I've lived through the day thus far,

I can live through another hour.

And then maybe you'll answer my prayer

and help my baby to sleep,

or my husband will take over,

or we can get someone to come in

so we can slip out.

Reprieved for a few hours, I'll be better able to continue

loving and caring for our fussy baby again.

Thank you, God, that there's always a way.

17

First Steps

You're doing great!
I'm more thrilled with your progress every day.
You grasp my fingers tightly and pull yourself up
to a sitting position,
>   chortling and laughing
>   as though to say,
>   "See what I can do!"
Soon your sturdy little legs will be supporting you.
A bit uncertainly to be sure,
but with audacious determination.
And then you'll venture forth,
>   laughing with glee,
>   as you drop my supporting fingers
>   and take your first steps alone.
You'll feed yourself,
>   your spoon finding your mouth somehow,
>   Your nearly empty bowl you'll dump on
>   the floor or on your head.
You'll hurl your bottle across the room
and announce your freedom from it,

You'll scale your Pack 'n Play and crib,
defying them to restrain you any longer.
Yes, my child,
you gloat over your small successes,
and so do I,
even as I pray
for wisdom
to plot your path of assuming responsibility
so you can tackle small tasks
 commensurate with your ability
 in order to know
 success upon success
 and achievement upon achievement.
You'll need this treasure trove of obstacles,
tackled and overcome, to give you
 the self-confidence
 and courage
 and assurance
 for more difficult tasks ahead.
The memory of achievements past
will light the flame
 of creative urge
 and enthusiasm
 to attempt even greater tasks.

So when failures come,
as failures surely will,

help me, O God, to perceive them lightly
and then to assure
my child of success
that is certain
to follow if we but persevere.
And conversely, make me
generous in affirmation of strengths revealed,
and genuine in praise and encouragement.

18

Loving With No
Expectation of Return

Today has been the most giving day.

My baby's been teething and is very fussy!

I was in tears when my husband came home at five o'clock.
He took the baby from my arms, brushed my forehead with a
kiss, and said, "Let's get a baby-sitter to come in for a couple of
hours so we can go out for a hamburger."

Oh, how wonderful!

"It's not that I don't love being with our baby…" I said later,
spooning ranch dressing on a gorgeous salad.

"Of course, hon. I know you do." He squeezed my hand.
"But caring for a baby requires a lot of time and effort and love.
And it all flows one way—from you to him."

"I suppose. But a baby has his own special way of rewarding
you. Those heart-stealing smiles, that warm, soft skin, the coos
and chuckles."

"It's still pretty one-sided," John said matter-of-factly, adding
catsup to his burger. "Especially when he's so young. And there

will be many more days like today, when he's teething or running a fever, or any number of things. Days when giving love is just that, with no expectation of return."

The words sent a little chill up my spine.

"The real test is when he gets a little older and wants to go against our rules and restraints," John went on. "Adolescence is a tough time for kids; they seem to feel a strong compulsion to declare their independence and can do some very foolish things."

"Like our neighbor's son," I said sadly. "I think he's tried just about everything. You might say, 'the complete package.'"

"Uh-huh." John replied pensively.

"I wonder if children are capable of destroying a parent's love for them," I asked. "Do you think it's possible?"

"If all a parent has is human love, I'm sure it is possible."

"It's scary, isn't it?"

John put down his burger and reached for my hand. "Without God it would be," he said solemnly. "But with His love, we can face whatever comes. He will pour His love into us and fill us to overflowing if we let Him."

"If we offer Him our empty hearts?"

"Empty hearts and eager spirits. He gives us a love that never gives up, that loves not because the object of our love is worthy, but because we can't help but love. If we love our child with this love, he will learn to love too. It's a challenge, but not impossible."

"It's a high goal."

"And we may never fully attain it. But we'll try." He picked up the check. "Let's go home to our fussy baby and love him for just the way he is."

Out in the parking lot I reached up and gave John a kiss.

"Thank you," I whispered. And in my heart I said, "Thank you, Lord!"

19

Doing the Mundane Tasks With Joy

It's time to clean again.
As long as you sleep peacefully, my sweet babe,
I'll be able to sail through my work,
    and a sparkling clean house will be my reward.
A few months from now
you won't sleep as much,
but spend your wakeful time
leaving a trail of toys behind you.
Books and magazines will be pulled from shelves in your
    search for who knows what.
And added to my weekly tasks of cleaning
will be hourly tasks of picking up
    and putting away.
I hope I'll be able to do it cheerfully.
I used to resent and dislike
    scrubbing toilets,
    scouring showers and tubs,
    dusting baseboards and

cleaning cupboards.
"Well," John says,
        "I wash the cars,
        sweep the garage,
        mow the lawn,
        and tackle the
always-flourishing,
indestructible weeds—
        and do repairs around the house.
That gets to be routine too."
We tried exchanging jobs,
        but that only worked for a day or two.
I guess deep down
I used to dream of the day when
        maybe—just maybe—our combined incomes
        would be enough
        to pay someone
to do all these tedious, repetitive chores that
        sometimes try me.
But then one day
we agreed that
routine tasks are what
        keep us in touch with reality,
        with the basic needs of life:
        food, clothing, shelter, transportation,
        and comfort.
We can live without the cultural enjoyments

and the luxuries of our affluent Western civilization,
but we can't live without
farmers,
homemakers,
builders,
and loving neighbors.
We must remember this.
Now I clean my house
with a song and a dance,
And I weed my garden without a guilty feeling that
I should be doing something more worthwhile.
John and I clean the garage together
and thank the Lord
for everyday
dusty, ho-hum, repetitive tasks
that keep us in touch with life as it really is.
This enhances our respect for those who spend
all their hours
providing for the rest of humanity:
food, clothing, shelter, transportation,
health care, and comfort.
The Lord Jesus spent His life that way.
I will too.
Joyfully.

20

I've Come to the Beach
This Morning

John is taking care of the baby, and I'm here on the beach again, Father.

It's so peaceful here, and I've been so busy!
And tired.

There are so many needs around us.
Heartaches. Problems. Loneliness. Despair. Crisis.

There is so much going on in people's lives!

They need you so badly, God.

I'm glad I've been able to help a few.

But sometimes I've been so busy I haven't taken time to refuel.

I snapped at John last night, and became impatient with my baby when he cried so hard and wouldn't stop.

Why do I act like that?

I feel like a hypocrite. I'm sweet to neighbors that call and grouchy to my own family.

So here I am, come to talk to you about it, Lord.

How could I have become so busy that I've forgotten to come back to my Source of refreshment?

I remember years ago underlining the words in Mark 3:13 that say, "Jesus...called to him those he wanted, and they came to him." As a young person it really meant a lot to me to think that you chose those you wanted to be with, and they wanted to be with you.

I found so much joy in fellowship and communion with you, God.

Then I got married, and suddenly life took on a new dimension. I was taken up with keeping our home clean and making meals and spending time with my husband. Then the baby came, and I wondered what I did with my time before. And now I wonder, will it ever be quiet and calm again?

I need to take time to be with you, dear God. Forgive me for not doing this. I need your help in disciplining myself. I need help in remembering what is most important. Too often I get busy with good things and omit taking time for the best.

I've come to the beach this morning, dear God, to get away from the telephone and the doorbell, and—yes—the baby, to tell you I'm sorry when I become impatient with my family. Forgive me. I do love you. Thank you again for John. And our baby.

And I love you, God, I really do. Help me be a better follower of yours. Amen.

And now I'll go home and get busy with the laundry, okay?

21

Firstborn

Our firstborn.

The first to learn to walk, to talk, to love.

The first to go to school.

To graduate. To go to college. Perhaps to marry.

A trailblazer.

Dear Lord, it's so important that he be a wise child!

We hope to have another child. In fact, we'd like to have four. We both love children, and we think we can provide for them and give them a good home. Are we wise, Lord, to try to bring up four little ones?

"Don't worry," Mom says. "Even if you only have two, there are lots of other children who need a home." I hadn't thought of that.

It means a lot to have our firstborn start out in the right direction, an example to others. O God, we pray especially for our firstborn.

May he grow in grace and truth, in wisdom and in love.

Give him a humble, teachable spirit.

A compassionate heart.

An industrious mind.

Common sense (not so common anymore).

Season him with good humor and fun and love of life.

He'll need patience and a forgiving spirit too.

He is very precious to us.

O God, look upon him with favor and bless him.

Amen.

22

Space to Grow

My Boston fern needs repotting.
When I lift it, the pot feels light.
I know it is all roots and very little soil.
I planted it in a narrow-mouthed Mexican pot,
    which I shall have to break
    to save the fern.
But I must do this,
    or the fronds will turn brown
    and the fern will shrink and die.
It needs fresh, moist soil
    and space to grow.
My creeping Charlie lost all its leaves
and withered and drooped,
until I lifted it from its confining pot
and gently transferred it to a big window box
    in a shady spot,
    where it has flourished like a tropical plant.

As I watch my baby grow,
I feel strange stirrings within me,

as though I've outgrown my space too
and become "root-bound."
I feel a need to break free,
to stretch and grow,
develop new skills,
discover hidden ones,
cultivate new friendships,
risk new patterns of life,
dare to question and read and examine
what I've drawn back from before, and
gather courage to accept and use all the strengths
and gifts God has given me.
I don't know if my husband will understand
this need to break the mold
and find fresh soil and space to grow;
to reach out to others and broaden my horizons.
Help him to understand, dear God.
Help me to know your will in this.

23

Thankfulness Begins With Me

I don't want my child to have a disgruntled outlook on life.

There is so much discontent, boredom, and unrest in the world today.

I want my child to be vibrant, confident, resourceful, and to overflow with gratitude and appreciation. Help me to be an example in this for him.

I know happiness and enthusiasm have a way of becoming infectious—like measles. But the reverse is also true. Grumbling and complaining are catchy.

If I can fill our home with song and laughter and joy, I know our children will be filled with joy too.

The disappointments of the day will slip away. Fatigue will drop off like a shed coat. Relationships will be tender, loving, responsive.

Father, help me to recover the enchantment a child knows with discovery. Help me see dew shimmering on a leaf, to feel with my bare toes the soft dampness of the earth, to raptly study

the journeys of ants and bugs, to be conscious of wind caressing my cheek and the sun warming my back, to smell the freshness of wet grass and rose blossoms after rain.

Set me free from slavery to time and chores so that I may watch with my child fluffy white clouds moving swiftly across the sky and quivering moonlight on lifted waves.

Teach me to cherish all those who love me and all those whom I love.

There's so much nagging and shouting. Some of it spills over our back fence. "You stupid idiot." "Oh, shut up! Quit your nagging." I hear demeaning comments even to the children. In supermarket aisles, I hear impatient moms: "Sit down!" "Stop that!" "No!" I don't want to be like that. Help me.

Help me to enjoy my daily work so my children will learn to help around the house cheerfully. I want them to bask in the warm feeling of having accomplished something worthwhile when the day is done.

And keep me, Lord, from complaining about the world we live in. Help me to put a positive spin on all that's going on around us.

Grant me a heightened awareness of life, that from it may flow a spontaneous gratitude for all things.

I know the thankfulness my child learns begins with me.

24

Ripples in Our Relationship

I thought the arrival of our first baby would bring the ultimate in happiness to my husband and me. I had pictured us as devoted parents, both hovering over the cradle. But I'm the one hovering over our sleeping newborn while my husband is checking school papers or off sailing in his dad's boat.

"Come with me on the boat today," he asked.

"But what will I do with the baby?"

"Bring him along."

"To the beach? On the water? It's windy. He'll get sunburned."

John snorted. "Babies aren't that fragile! We can rent an umbrella."

I didn't go, and I wish I had. I had an awful day!

I didn't eat lunch at noon, and later made a huge ice cream sundae with fudge sauce and cashews.

My baby slept all day, except for his feeding times. It was actually quite boring! I toyed with thoughts of my husband spending more time at home with me—if he really loved me.

I called my mom after my husband left for work on

Monday and told her what a horrid Sunday I'd had.

She listened and was silent.

"Well?" I said.

I could hear her draw a deep breath.

"Sue," she said, "I don't think John is neglecting you. I think you're neglecting him. Just because you enjoy being a mother doesn't mean you should neglect being a wife."

"I can't believe you don't understand me better than that!" I said.

After our brief conversation was over, I felt more miserable than ever.

I called my best friend and told her my troubles. She almost always understands.

"Well, Sue," she said briskly, "maybe you'd better start going with John when he asks you to, or he might stop asking you."

Wow! What kind of a friend is that! I thought. *She just doesn't get it!*

The past two weeks have been miserable. John and I have either quarreled or sat silently through a whole meal.

We've gone to bed back to back every night. One night I found John sitting in the rocker in the dark. "What on earth are you doing?" I asked.

"Thinking."

He sounded as miserable as I felt. I almost gave in, but then an inner voice said, "You have nothing to apologize for," so I was silent.

What has happened to us? We used to be so much in love, so happy!

I couldn't stand it any longer, so I took the baby and went home to Mom and Dad. Mother was out, but Dad was there when I arrived.

"I've been thinking I should move back home," I told him.

"Oh?" Dad sounded mildly surprised. "Well, I think we would have to advise you to go right back to your husband. John's a fine young man. You must have thought so too, or you wouldn't have married him. What seems to be the trouble?"

We talked then, and finally Dad said, "You know, Sue, in order to have a happy marriage your mother and I have discovered two things: we both have to forgive, and we both have to learn to be interested in what the other enjoys."

"Oh," I said.

Dear Lord, I need your help more than I ever have before. I'm too proud to ask forgiveness. Can you help me overcome my pride? Can you help me tell John I'm sorry I've been so self-centered and stubborn?

I called on the Lord, and He heard me and answered me.

I apologized to John when he got home. He kissed me and said, "Will you go with me next Saturday?"

"I'd love to," I said.

And somehow I know I will.

25

Sometimes Loving Means Disciplining

"You only have I known of all the families of the earth; therefore, I will punish you for all your iniquities" (Amos 3:2 KJV).

"Thus says the Lord to this people, 'Even so they have loved to wander; they have not kept their feet in check. Therefore the Lord does not accept them; now He will remember their iniquity and call their sins to account'" (Jeremiah 14:10 NASB).

These words captured my attention when I read them during my quiet time this morning.

The word *known* in Amos 3:2 is the word used to describe the most intimate relationship between a husband and wife.

God's bond with the people of Israel was that close. He loved them that much.

But these verses tell me more. Because God loved them so dearly God said He had to visit them. He had to say to them,

"Now what have you been doing?" He didn't wink at their sin. He made them accountable for what they had done. They had to learn to take responsibility for their choices and their acts. In other words, He had to discipline them. He had to discipline them because He loved them.

It won't take too long before our little one will begin to disobey. He'll probably try to tell lies, to get by with things he has done.

Then we'll have to call him to account. Not let him get by. See to it that he accepts responsibility for what he has done.

That's not going to be easy. He'll test us. He'll deny wrongdoing. He'll do everything he can to get away with whatever wrong he has done. He'll try to wear us down so we give up.

We'll need to become skilled in knowing how to make him accept the consequences of his actions. If he doesn't learn as a child, he'll continue his behavior as an adult, and that will only lead to more trouble.

Dear God, it takes so much wisdom to be a parent! Disciplining in the right way is particularly difficult. Help us to learn from books, from seminars, and from other parents. And when we fail, forgive us. Above all, help us to keep our relationship with our child warm and loving as he grows up. Please help us, dear God.

26

A Father's Delight

I love to watch my husband when he plays with our child.

The lines in his face, taut from the day's work, begin to soften.

His eyes grow tender with love.

His face actually beams.

His big hands gently handle our baby. He holds our little one close to his own strong body.

He brushes his stubbly cheek against the downy head.

Obligingly he closes his mouth on the tiny fingers that explore his mouth.

When our baby finds his daddy's eyeball, Dad softly chides, "Hey, you! That's out of bounds!"

Chuckles and laughter spill.

The love my husband exudes bathes us all.

I am so proud of my husband! He is already a good father.

Maybe he doesn't think about it, but his happy face is making an impression on our baby, reassuring him that he is loved, wanted, and cherished by his father.

There is no greater gift we can give our child.

I'm so glad that my husband freely expresses his delight in his baby son!

27

I Wanted to Breast-Feed My Baby

I was disappointed.

I had hoped so much to be able to breast-feed you through the first year, my little one. But you're so hungry. And my supply just isn't enough.

The disappointment was so acute it spilled over into tears in the doctor's office.

The doctor is young, and I think he was a bit embarrassed about my tears.

"I wouldn't let it get you down, Sue. Eighteen years from now when your son's playing quarterback, no one's going to ask him if he was breast- or bottle-fed."

The idea was so preposterous I burst out laughing. It sure helps to keep things in perspective.

I hope I can continue to do so. I can foresee the questions I'll be tempted to ask.

I wonder if this kid will ever be potty-trained. And the answer I'll probably get from Mom: "I haven't met a man yet who isn't."

Do you think he will ever give up dragging around his blanket? "I haven't seen a school kid doing it, have you?"

Spilled milk again! Will we ever get past having milk spilled? "Probably not," John may say, "but it's only milk, and we can always wipe it up."

Mother said the other day that our concerns will grow as our children grow. I can guess what she meant by that.

"Your son is too rough on the playground."

"Your son is failing math."

"Your son has totaled the car!"

"Your son is on drugs." Not that, I hope!

For now, I'm going to be thankful that my problems are only small ones, like my not being able to breast-feed you all the time.

Here's your bottle, you hungry little thing. You sure love milk, don't you? And I can still cuddle you and hold you close and talk to you and sing. The loving and cuddling are the most important anyway.

As for the bigger problems, I'll leave those until they come, one by one. With God's help I think we'll make it through those too.

28

Peek-a-Boo!

We play peek-a-boo, you and I. You chortle and chuckle. Your whole face breaks out into smiles; your arms and legs, your whole body trembles and responds with joy. Looking at you, my heart fills with happiness. I cover my face again, staying behind the blanket longer than usual, then, "Peek-a-boo!" I cry and your whole body jumps in gleeful response.

Peek-a-boo is fun now, but do I want you to play peek-a-boo your whole life through? It all depends.

If peek-a-boo means retaining a certain quality of mystery, exposing some unknown facet of your personality or nature to your friends, then let's continue playing peek-a-boo. Later in life when you find a new friend or meet your spouse, you'll understand that it's the joy of discovery of all the delightful qualities of that friend that is so exciting. As you seek to know someone better, it's like a game of peek-a-boo. Occasionally we act in unexpected ways or say unexpected things. We free parts of ourselves that may have been bound before, giving wings to our dreams or briefly letting go of our inhibitions.

"I never knew Janie had that in her!" a friend will exclaim.

But to have adequate resources to draw from to mystify and charm means to continually grow. I watch you yawn and stretch, and I am happy about your growth. I want you to continue to grow in body and in spirit.

To be insatiably curious. To daringly explore. Becoming more and more the whole person God wants you to be. Then you'll shine and reveal facets of yourself to your friends. Traits they haven't seen before that will enchant and fascinate them.

But peek-a-boo in the sense of covering up—this is not what we want for you, little one. We want you to grow up being free to be *you*. Not like the other children in our family, not like your cousins, not even like other children you might hear us admire. We want you to be the true person that you are. You are unique. There is no one in the world like you.

Yesterday the girl next door dropped in. "I can hardly wait until after my wedding day so I can be myself again," she confessed.

Oh, my! Don't ever pretend like that. You'll never be happy if you do. You'll be tense, worried, and even deceptive.

Masquerading as someone you are not can get you into big trouble and can only lead to unhappiness.

To enable the true you to burst from its cocoon and emerge a beautiful butterfly, Dad and I will try our best to be ourselves. We'll let you see our worst with our best, at the same time as you see us forgiving, loving, accepting, and being reconciled over and over again.

Peek-a-boo! It's a harmless baby game now. When you are mature, it is a game that can either enrich or destroy. Be genuine, little one, and a lot of fun. Enrich and delight.

29

Your Child Will Come to Know God Through You

"Your child will learn to know God through you," the pastor said Sunday in his sermon.

That scared me.

I'm not good enough for my child to get a picture of God through me.

I make mistakes. I sin every day.

The idea bothered me so much that when I found myself sitting next to our pastor at the Sunday school teachers' appreciation dinner that evening, I blurted out my fears to him.

"Oh, no!" he said, placing his hand over mine. "I should have explained better what I meant."

"You are an example of God to your child. You love him, care for him tenderly. You feed him, bathe him, change him, soothe him when he is upset or sick or teething. You get a baby-sitter to care for him when you're out. You'd never abandon your child."

I smiled. I was beginning to understand.

"Through your love, your child will come to understand God's love for him. He will also grow in his understanding of God as you teach and discipline him."

"That's what I worry about," I said. "I know I'll make mistakes. I'll scold him when he isn't deserving of it, or I'll be too permissive or too harsh. And I'll lose my temper—I know I will! How will he learn about God through that?"

My pastor chuckled. "When he gets older, he'll learn that God works through imperfections. Besides," he leaned back in his chair, "remember that while your child will come to know God through you, God isn't limited to working through you. He'll work through other people too. He'll reveal himself to your child through His Word, both as you teach it and later as your child studies it for himself. And your child will learn to know God as he experiences Him in worship and in prayer; in tension and in conflict; in joy and in crises. God has many ways of introducing himself to people. He doesn't expect you to do it all. So relax. Stop worrying about the mistakes you fear you'll make. And concentrate instead on showing steadfast love to your child. Does that make it easier?"

I blinked rapidly to hold back the tears. *I can do that*, I thought.

30

Teething

You're having a hard time with your new teeth coming in, my precious baby, and I'll do all I can to relieve and comfort you.

Life has its troubles, heartaches, and disappointments. Could teething be a small foreshadowing of what life has in store? One of the most important lessons we can teach you will be to bear up under troubles with courage and grace.

It won't be easy. It's only natural to want to shield our loved ones from pain and disappointment. To protect to a certain degree is right and even needful. Children are not adults and were never meant to carry adult-sized burdens. But at the same time, they must be conditioned little by little to carry loads. If their muscles aren't strengthened and developed gradually, a man-sized load dropped on their unprepared shoulders could be a real shock.

But how much disappointment and trouble we can put in your scales without tipping them will require heavenly wisdom. Some calamities, of course, we can't prevent—much as we would like to! But how we allow you to handle the daily small upsets is what's important.

Your older cousin Kyle seems to understand this almost intuitively. Yesterday your two-year-old cousin, Jack, walking on the outside railing of the deck, fell into the rosebushes. He lay crying, unable to kick out his anger because of the thorns all around him. Kyle came out, surveyed the situation, and said, "Well, pick yourself up, Jack!"

So, my precious one, I won't run frantically every time you fall and cry. You'll have to learn to pick yourself up! Later the lessons will be harder to learn. You may lose a pet. Your bicycle may be broken. Then it will be hard for me to prepare you—to refrain from replacing your pet immediately or rushing to buy you a new bike.

Life will require that you grieve if you are to be healed. I must permit you to grieve, to suffer loss, to know emptiness, to feel anguish. For life will present you with some irreplaceable losses, when you'll have to settle for second bests.

O heavenly Father, just thinking of all the wisdom and strength required of me to prepare my child to accept and bear loss drives me to you. I need your help, your whispered coaching in my ear, your strong assurance as I watch my child suffer, that in the end it will bear the worthy fruit of preparation.

31

No Time for a Quiet Time

Whoosh! Four whole days have zipped by without my finding five free minutes to sit down with my Bible.

The baby's been sick. Company came. My husband has been down with the flu. I feel cross-eyed with weariness.

I wonder how many times I've run up and down those stairs today. Or how many times I got up last night.

I've been too tired to read or even to pray. I told the Lord about it last night as I cried into the kitchen sink, feeling a little sorry for myself.

"It's all right," He seemed to say. *"You should know by now our relationship isn't dependent on how much you read or pray. Our relationship won't change. It's just that if you can find a few moments to come before me and to meditate on my Word, I can refresh you and bring you new strength. 'In returning and in rest will be your confidence.'"*

This refreshment, this heavenly energy is what I need, dear God. My own natural resources have been exhausted. Quiet my heart. Relax my taut muscles and loosen the band of pressure around my head. Pour into me your rejuvenating power of the Resurrection that I may have the strength to carry on. Thank you, God. You are an ever-faithful God.

32

Crossing Bridges

Many new experiences await us, my child.

In the years to come we'll learn to build bridges of understanding between us and you. And in crossing those bridges, we'll often get tired and be tempted to just give up.

Especially if you are an enthusiastic person who questions and probes.

Times change. And your dad and I will *try* to change with them. But it's hard to keep pace with the younger generation. Maybe in some instances it's best not to try.

When you start asking questions about why we do things the way we do, we'll be middle-aged! It's a scary thought.

If you're full of vision and new ideas, as I hope you will be, you may sometimes feel like nothing is being done in the community, in the world.

That will come as an insult to us, because we all need to feel that our lives have been worthwhile; that the world is a better place because *we've* been here.

From your perspective, you'll only see what remains to be done, and I do hope you will make your mark in the world.

But we'll need those bridges of understanding between you and us so we can still love and cherish one another. And if we get tired of trying, I hope you'll understand and be patient with us.

These are strange thoughts to be having as I hold you, my little babe in arms.

Since you were born I've been able to see more clearly the bridges my parents have tried to build to reach me.

I've remembered too the times I stood at the other end of the bridge and yelled impatiently at them, "What's wrong with you?"

I feel bad now when I remember those times. Why didn't *I* try to build a bridge? Or when my parents did, why didn't I meet them halfway?

And now I look at you, cradled in my arms, so soft and sweet and innocent. I wonder if someday when you hurt me, intentionally or not, I'll be strong enough to build a bridge.

I hope so.

O God, you who are the source of all wisdom, give me the understanding and patience I shall need in the years ahead. Teach me the lessons I need to learn day by day.

33

Father God, Forgive, Restrain

O merciful and forgiving heavenly Father,
I feel so awful.
I didn't set out to hurt my baby; but
    suddenly I was so angry.
I never knew it was possible to be that angry.
It was terrible!
I have no excuses either,
    because I know
    no matter how much my baby cries,
    no matter how tired I am,
    no matter how many frustrations the day has
        brought,
    I must never, *ever* hurt my child.
Thank you, God, that you kept me from it.
Thank you that you gave me the sense to put my baby
    in his crib
    where he would be safe.
And then, somehow—I don't remember how—

I found myself in the next room
crying and crying
until I could cry no more,
and I was quiet inside.
But I've discovered my potential to feel anger toward
my helpless, innocent child
whom I love so dearly,
and it is frightening.
O God, I humbly ask that
you will protect us both,
my child from harm
and me from doing something
that will leave me with memories
that sear and haunt.
O merciful God,
the task of being a parent is so demanding.
Please help me to do it well.
Guide me each day in this most holy task.

34

Heated Exchange

My husband is dedicated to thorough research and almost, I think, inordinately insistent upon accuracy. He's been working for months on his thesis for his M.A. He writes and rewrites. Checks and double-checks. At the rate he's going, our child will probably graduate from high school before John gets his degree. I know that's an exaggeration, and I *am* glad he is a meticulous scholar, but it seems like it's taking forever.

"Sometimes you exasperate me!" I exploded at him. I had wanted to go out for the evening last night, but he was pecking out another draft of chapter three.

Usually John takes my frank eruptions in silence. Yesterday, however, he looked up from his typewriter and answered back with, "Well, sometimes you annoy me too!"

It was so unexpected that my spontaneous reaction was to laugh. He looked at me, incredulous, and then his grin snapped the final thread of tension between us.

How good, I thought later, that we are learning to speak openly to each other, because we are growing in mutual trust. I know I shouldn't express my annoyance every time I feel myself beginning to bristle. There's a place for self-control, after all. But once in a while it's good to let the pressure escape, confident that a loving heart will sift through what I say, heeding what is worthwhile and quietly discarding the rest. How good not to have to weigh every word or to speak cautiously so as to be assured we are saying the right thing—in the opinion of our listener, that is.

Frank exchange of ideas and opinions lie ahead for *us* too, my child.

The differences between *us* may well be even greater than the ones between your dad and me right now.

Your dad and I chose each other. You didn't choose us, and in one sense, we didn't choose you either.

But we can come to an understanding as we learn to talk freely with each other, sharing emotions and reactions as well as ideas.

Dad and I will keep on practicing the art of communication, so that you will grow up in an atmosphere where sharing freely, without fear, will seem as natural as eating and sleeping.

35

Choices

I look at you and smile when I think of the choices you will have to make in the near future. They aren't big ones, but to learn and grow you will have to make them.

Like deciding whether you want the Cheerios clutched in your hand or your hand free of the plastic container you are pulling them out of. You'll never get your hand out as long as you grasp the Cheerios in your fist. The top just isn't big enough.

Of course, if you weren't so frustrated, maybe you'd listen to me. Tip the container over and let the Cheerios fall onto the table. Oh, you catch on fast! Did you really understand what I said, or did you figure it out on your own?

The time will come when you'll discover you can't have two things at once; you'll have to make a choice. Which do you want more? The sooner you learn this lesson the better. Of course, you'll never be finished learning. I have to relearn it myself sometimes. Like when I gain a few pounds. I must say no to pizza and shakes, and all kinds of other good things. It's a lesson in life all of us have to learn. Choices. Decisions. You can't have everything. Sometimes the choice is between better and best.

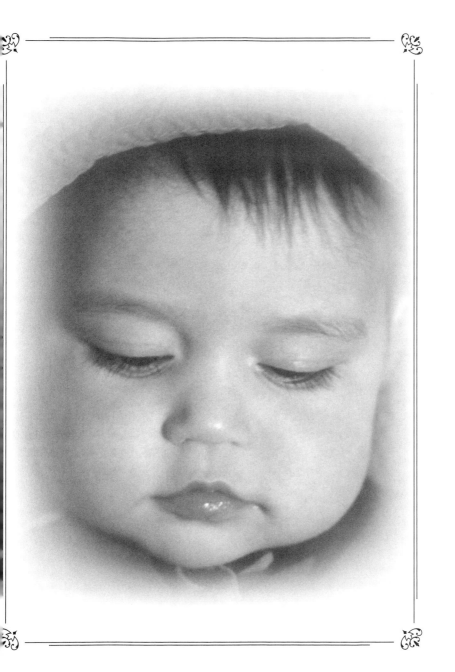

When we abandon what we want so much, we find freedom; and later, what we wanted may drop into our hand as well.

It was like that for me when I was trying to get pregnant. John and I wanted so much to have a child, but even though we tried and tried, nothing happened. And then I gave up.

"All right, Lord," I said. "I don't understand it, but if you don't want us to have children for some reason, I can accept that."

Of course, it wasn't easy, and I cried a lot.

And wouldn't you know it, not long after that I discovered I was expecting a baby! I had opened my fist and let go. I found freedom and got my heart's desire too.

You look so solemn as you sit there eating your Cheerios one by one. I know you don't really understand what I'm telling you, but I'll keep on trying to explain and show you through *my* choices. Someday you too will understand.

36

I'm Trying to Do It On My Own

I can see where it's going to be a little difficult. My ideas and my mother's just aren't the same when it comes to raising children.

I love my mother, and I don't want to hurt her. I believe she did a good job bringing up her children. I have a good self-image, and I like my brothers and sisters. But I still think there's room for improvement.

I don't want to spend as much time caring for the house as my mom did. At least, I don't think that way right now. A messy room really does not upset me.

I want to encourage my child to try difficult things, even if he messes up the house in the process.

We actually differ in a number of ways.

But shouldn't I have the courage to follow what my husband and I think is right? Isn't that what is meant by leaving your father and mother to cleave to your spouse?

Dear God, can you help my mother understand this? Can you help her let go of me and let me raise my child the way I see fit? Can you give us the wisdom and understanding we need to do a good job of caring for a family?

I know we're young, but with your help, our youth shouldn't keep us from doing what is right. I want this family to be uniquely ours. Amen.

37

Thank You for My Husband

Last night I thought I had reached the end of my rope. The third night up with a fussy, sick baby is a little too much. I was sitting in the rocker, holding my restless, feverish bundle when John padded down the stairs.

"Can I help you?" His tired look told me it took real effort for him to get up and ask me that.

"I don't think anyone can help, John. Go back to bed. You have to go to work tomorrow."

"Are you sure I can't help?"

"Yes, I'm sure."

He creaked up the stairs again, but when I heard our bedroom door shut, the tears began to fall.

How miserable, utterly miserable, being a mother when there is nothing you can do to make your child happy! And I was so tired. How would I ever be able to struggle through tomorrow? I wondered.

The tears fell faster than ever. Then I heard the door open, and the stairs creak again. This time John had his warm robe wrapped around him and he was wearing his slippers.

"I figured even if I can't do anything, I could at least just sit here with you."

What a treasured moment!

My tears stopped.

The fatigue was gone.

My moist eyes mutely thanked him.

And half an hour later the baby fell asleep.

Thank you, God, for my husband.

38

Sheer Joy

We've got a good thing going between us, you and I,
    a warm, intimate, trusting relationship,
    bringing immeasurable joy.
    You cuddle up,
    nuzzling your chin into my neck,
    burying your nose in my hair.
Then you raise your head,
    pull away,
    and look deeply into my eyes,
    yours alive with innocent mischief,
    your mouth forming an O as you ooh and aah.
Our eyes seem fixed on each other,
    and I think I have never known such joy.
I hold you close.
How much happiness you bring to our home!
It can't get better than this.
How will I contain it if it does?
We've got a good thing going between us, you and I,
    a warm, intimate, trusting relationship.

May it always be so, my precious little one.

Oh, Lord, let this bond continue to grow and grow and sustain us during any difficulties that may lie ahead.

39

My Baby Was Very Sick

I shouldn't have worried so much, but I did when our baby got sick. I was almost frantic.

What do you do when such a small child gets so sick? He can't tell you a thing. I hate to think what it would be like if I couldn't call our doctor.

But we *do* have a good doctor to call, and the medicine our baby needed was available. In a couple of days he was well again.

Now that it's all over, I feel silly that I worried about it so much. I also am ashamed that I forgot to thank God for all the help that is available to us.

It is easy to worry when you are a new mother and you naturally feel so protective of your baby and so responsible for all his care. But we can be so thankful that we live where help is close and doctors and nurses and pharmacists are kind and helpful.

We do thank you, O God, for this. We thank you also that ultimately you are our healer.

We think of all in this world who do not have expert, professional care when they become ill. Forgive us for not doing more to help them. Stand beside and bless all those around the world who try to care for the sick and dying. In Jesus name, amen.

40

Not Really Mine

Bone of my bone
and flesh of my flesh,
an extension of your daddy and me.
That's you, my little one.
Small wonder, then, that I love you.
For to love you is,
in reality, to love myself.
But that's all right too,
for God intended that we love ourselves,
that we feel good about who we are.
Only I must recognize
that in this close tie
two dangers lurk.
One, that even though you are part of me,
   I must learn to release you
   and know that you are not really
   mine,
   or your daddy's,
   or ours together,

but you belong to God.
Because of this,
I must understand also
that you do not feel as closely bound to me,
or ever will, as I do to you.

When the cord that bound you to me was severed,
you lost your sense
of ever having been part of me.
You feel you are only you,
and that is enough.
I know this to be true
because I think of my relationship with my mother
and know that, though I love her dearly,
I feel no dependency upon her,
nor do I want her to feel she must be anxious for me.
I am complete as I am, apart from her,
and I can exist alone.
I say this not out of arrogant pride
but rather to ease her burden.
This too I must remember
as I seek to develop your independence from me.
In a sense you are already free from me,
even though you will grow and grow
in more responsible freedom.
And as you do, I will never cease to care—

I cannot—love cannot,
but I can learn to release and trust you to God,
    who loves you dearly,
and not to worry.
At least not too much.

41

I Love You Just As You Are

Baby:

You are important to me.

Valuable.

Worthwhile.

You can't do a thing yet except demand attention
and care from me.

Yet I love you.

Deeply.

Passionately.

I love you for yourself.

For what you are now—a squirming, helpless, sometimes
happy, sometimes cranky bundle of humanity.

Your presence fills our home with happiness.

I love you and enjoy you for what you are *now*

not for what you will become.

And understanding that this is the way I love you makes

it easier for me to understand and believe

that this is the way God loves me—

right now. Just the way I am.

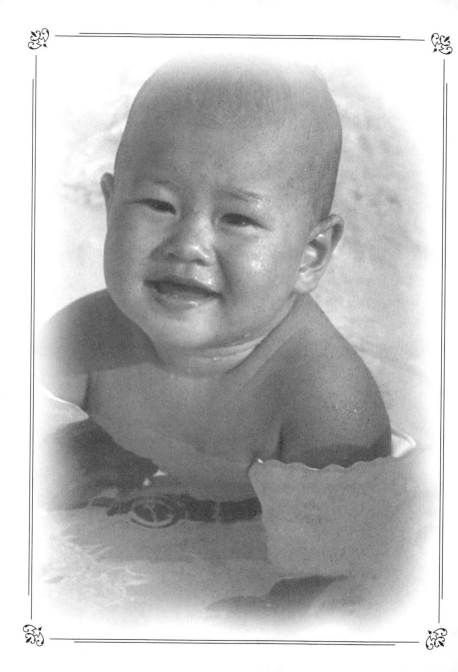

42

I Am a Good Mother

As I look at you, my child, now several months old,
     I feel so proud.
Your sturdy little body is a picture of health
     and strength.
Your bright eyes take in your world,
     your hands explore,
     your legs kick with abandon.
You yell with passion,
     pull hair mercilessly, and
     smile engagingly.
I look at you and think,
     the best thing I've done so far in life
     is give birth to this baby!
I think I'm a good mother.

Our house smells sweet and fresh.
"I'd dreaded having a baby,"
your dad confided the other night,
"because I'd been in some homes that reeked of diapers
and soiled clothes.

I couldn't face the thought.
I don't know how you've done it,
but our house and baby always smell fresh."
"I'm a good mother," I said, smiling coyly.

I'm learning to trust a baby-sitter with you
once in a while
so your daddy and I can have time together,
or I can have time alone.

I think I'm a good mother because I love and cherish.
If I had to account for all my faults,
*   my head would droop,*
*   my song would die,*
*   my feet would drag*
But you, dear God, forgive me
*   for Jesus' sake,*
and constantly cleanse me.
And this, I believe, my children will know one day:
*   that deep down,*
*   I love you, God,*
*   and want to walk in your way.*
And they will know
*   my love for them too.*
Knowing all my shortcomings,
I can still say and truly believe:
I am a good mother.

43

Sometimes It's Hard to Live With Plenty

I don't expect my child will ever know hunger that is not satisfied—I pray that he will not!

But he will live in a world where hunger is the everyday experience of increasing millions.

If I had lived all my life in North America, and if I had never seen bloated bellies with umbilical hernias and huge, vacant, staring eyes, or legs and arms that are mere bony sticks covered over with parched brown skin, I would find it hard to believe that people actually die of hunger around the world.

But I have seen the outstretched hand, the listless shuffling, grown men curled up in fetal positions on the pavement—dying.

I have seen human beings behave like animals—clawing each other for a scrap of bread found in a trash heap.

I look at the beautiful clothing my baby has and wonder why my child and I are so blessed.

We could just as well have been born into poverty in a country where there is so little hope for anything more.

I am truly rich—in so many ways. And so is my child.

O God, instill in us a willingness to help your impoverished children. Give us the hunger that cannot be satisfied except by doing your will.

Have mercy on us, God!

Sometimes it's hard,

so very hard

to have so much!

44

I Want My Child
to Love Books

The joy of discovery.
Help me to enable my child to experience this again and
    again.
Children are naturally curious.
    Adults stifle this curiosity
    by countless restrictions and prohibitions
    because of fear;
    by ignoring the child or giving meaningless answers.
Help me, Lord, to allow my child's curiosity to lead him to
the joy of discovery—
through questions,
    experiments,
    observations,
    and through books.
Oh, Lord, help him find the joy of reading good books.
Many have been robbed of the adventure in reading by
the magnetic appeal of TV.
May our child not be one of them.

May he treasure the art of reading,

value the opportunities that are his to learn to read,

appreciate the wealth stored in libraries for him.

I covet for our child an eagerness to learn!

Help me to set aside more time to read to him

books that will entertain,

delight,

fascinate,

arouse curiosity,

answer questions and raise others;

books that will cause him at the end to flip back to the front
page and say eagerly, "Read it again!"

And may I remember to include the Book that can lead him to
the greatest discovery of all: his Lord and Savior Jesus Christ.

45

A Dream of Shared Privilege and Responsibility

John came home last night,
    slumped into a chair,
    and sat staring.
At dinner he picked at his food,
    and when the baby began to cry,
    he looked pained.
    He excused himself,
    and headed for our bedroom.
My stomach feels like dried out play dough
when John comes home so tired.
I wistfully wish things could be different.
I dream sometimes
    of a life
    where both of us would work part time,
    and have the rest of the time to share in
    caring for our children,
    for our home, and in
reaching out to areas of need

in our community;
enriching our lives,
developing a better relationship
with each other,
with others,
and with God.
Sometimes I think dreamily
that if we both could have trained
for the same vocation
and shared the same job,
we could more easily empathize
and better understand each other.
Of course, temptations to competition and envy could
arise.
We would have to deal with those.
And I suppose it isn't very realistic for most couples
to think in these terms,
and maybe not even desirable.
For possessing varied skills
and working at different vocations
can enrich our lives,
widen our interests,
and season our conversation.
But wouldn't it be possible
for both of us to work part time?
We're not greedy for money.
We don't have to have two salaries,

or the possessions two salaries can buy.
The simple life contents us.
So if couples could divide their working hours,
and husbands could be more relaxed and not as tired,
think what it could mean

    to wives,

    to children,

    to churches,

    to homes,

    to all the needy areas of life.
And think what it could mean to discontented,
frustrated wives
to be able

    to bud and bloom,

    sprout and grow,

    discover and develop,

    study and put to use

    all that lies latent within them.
Would it mean too, I wonder,

    fewer heart attacks,

    fewer ulcers,

    better all-around health and humor,

    and more fully developed relationships

    between husbands and wives,

    parents and children,

    families and the outside world,

    people and God?

Wistfully, I think all this and wonder
if the day will come.
If not for us, perhaps for our child?

46

Prayer of a Working Mother

All day long I have mourned and grieved
for tomorrow is the day I must leave my child
in the care of another.
My little one doesn't know it,
but I do, and wonder,
what will he think tomorrow
when I drop him off
and don't come back in an hour or so to pick him up?
Does he understand time?
Does he know how long
four, five, or six hours is?
Will he grow anxious, restless, miss me, cry?
Or, as the days pass, learn to love another
more than me?
Will he care when finally, at night,
weary I return
to hold him close, to stroke his hair,
to bury my nose in his neck,
to love him and love him and love him?
O God, how happy I am to be a mother.

But oh how it hurts tonight!
Hear my cry, O Lord.
Bind up the wounds of my heart,
ease my pain, dry my tears,
and help me to lean hard on you.
And cradle our little one in your strong arms,
that he may feel loved and secure.

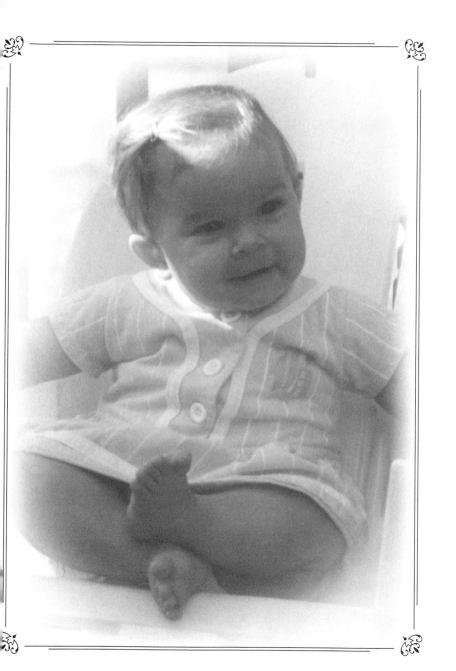